# UNMASKING THE TRAUMA

*School Bullying and Children with Special Needs*

A Compilation Presented by
April J. Lisbon, EdD

Foreword by Sabrina Thomas

© 2018 April J. Lisbon

*Unmasking the Trauma: School Bullying and Children with Special Needs*

First Edition, October 2018

Fredericksburg, VA

Running Your Race Publishers

www.advocacycoaching.com

Editing: Shayla Raquel, ShaylaRaquel.com

Cover Design: GraphixMotion, GraphixMotionMedia.com

Interior Formatting: GraphixMotionMedia.com

*Unmasking the Trauma: School Bullying and Children with Special Needs* is under copyright protection. No part of this book may be used or reproduced in any manner whatsoever without written permission except in the case of brief quotations embodied in critical articles and reviews. Printed in the United States of America. All rights reserved.

ISBN: 978-0-9998493-1-6

❦ Created with Vellum

*This book is dedicated to all parents and educators who have witnessed and experienced the trauma of bullying against children with special needs in K-12 education.*

*To my son, Jerel, I honor you in this moment for your bravery in the face of adversity. You gave me courage to compile this book during our darkest hours. I thank you and I love you, son.*

# FOREWORD

## by Sabrina Thomas

I connected with April J. Lisbon through autism. We both have sons with autism, and we both are very involved parents and advocates of the condition.

Having disabilities can raise other concerns like being in social settings and developing relationships with other people. It can also be a cause of conflicts among children. Serious issues, like bullying, deserve attention. As a mother of a special needs son, I often worry about him being bullied, because children can get victimized for various reasons. Just the thought of my son being attacked in that way is very disturbing. Even though I never had a personal situation with my son and bullying, I have very strong feelings about school bullying or bullying of any kind.

So what is school bullying? School bullying is a type of bullying that occurs in any educational setting. School bullying is a hostile intent, distress, repetition, and provocation. Bullying can have a wide spectrum of effects on a student, such as depression, anger, stress, and even suicide. Most of the time, this type of bullying is done on the school bus, in the classrooms, and in locker rooms. Also, the bully can develop different social disorders or have a higher chance of criminal activity.

Bullying is a very serious problem. Kids are being victimized every day physically and verbally. Children with physical, developmental, intellectual, emotional, and sensory disabilities are at an increased risk for bullying.

As I read through each chapter, I needed a break after each one because of all the emotions that welled up inside of me. I wondered if that were me, what would I have done? Each chapter has a heartfelt story of a special needs child experiencing bullying, and each story is different but powerful.

There were many times I wondered if my son was bullied. I had a few conversations with him and his teachers throughout the years when he had behavioral changes. I always wanted to rule out bullying first. I often wondered if he would even understand what it meant to be bullied. Because my son is nonverbal for the most part, he would have a difficult time explaining a situation to me. It is hard for a special needs parent to figure out what is happening to their child, especially if the child doesn't speak or has limited social skills. As parents of special needs children, we really need to connect with our children, especially to those who cannot speak. These authors were connected to their children and immediately noticed a difference in their behaviors and trusted their gut.

In the pages of this book, you will discover what advocacy really means. After I read each chapter, one thing resonated with me: they all had the three A's. Each author's chapter was about advocacy, awareness, and action. You will learn the steps each author took to resolve their personal situation. These stories also share how to become an advocate for your child or loved one so they receive the best care possible. Responding quickly to bullying is so important.

After reading all the authors' stories, I feel empowered that if I had a bullying situation, I would be better equipped. I also know of additional resources. Each author's action and how they stepped in truly moved me.

Have your pen and paper ready to jot down tips and strategies. You will be encouraged and inspired by their strength and persistence.

Have you ever wondered if your child has been bullied, or are you struggling with that thought right now? I'll be honest: that is always on my mind. Just keep reading; these chapters will move you. This book not only shares each author's journey and experience in bullying, but also educates you. The authors in *Unmasking the Trauma* bring you along on their journey so you're experiencing the moment with them.

Thank you, April J. Lisbon, for being the visionary for this anthology. Thank you for all that you do in the autism and special needs community.

Thank you to all the authors for sharing your stories and for being authentic. This book is meant to spread awareness regarding bullying. Also, this book shows how parents love and fight for their children.

Parents and caregivers, we always have to advocate for our

children. No one is going to love them more, keep them safe, and fight for more than we will.

---

*"Attacking someone with disabilities is the lowest display of power I can think of."*
—*Morgan Freeman*

---

Sabrina Thomas
   Speaker, Advocate & Author
   Virginia Beach, VA
   www.sabrinatspeaks.com

# INTRODUCTION

Bullying is a chronic issue today in schools. It involves targeted humiliation and intimidation of a person who is physically or socially stronger than the victim. Specifically, bullying is designed to make the victim feel powerless.[1] What's most disturbing about the issues of bullying in schools to date is that in Western culture, 9–25 percent of school-age children are victims of bullying.[2]

Unfortunately, bullying in schools impacts the learning environment of students. According to Dupper, "Victims of chronic bullying have poorer grades, increased rates of truancy, increased rates of dropping out, loss of self-esteem, and feelings of isolation and depression, and some even attempt suicide."[3] For those with special needs, it's even more traumatic. Children with special needs often face peer rejection, have social skills deficits, have fewer friends, and are at risk of being isolated within an inclusion setting model.[4] For individuals diagnosed with higher functioning autism, for example, "The vast majority of children with Asperger's disorder (89 percent) experienced victimization in their lifetime compared to children with autistic disorder (49 percent) or other ASDs (60 percent)."[5]

With so many state regulations and school-based programs to help *combat* issues related to bullying, why hasn't the number of bullying cases declined in recent years? What's happening in our schools? Why are more and more families, especially those of children with special needs, being subjected to such harassment in our schools?

Enough is enough. As parents and educators, we desire that all children can attend schools where they are accepted for their unique differences. As parents and educators, we know that mocking an individual's physical or mental limitations is a form of bullying. However, as we have seen in recent years, even individuals who hold high-ranking positions of authority in our society will mock individuals who are different than they are.[6] Sometimes, they will even deny that the offense ever occurred. But the victim feels it and may experience this hurt for days, months, or even years after the offense(s) has occurred. Is it now safe to assume that it's an *acceptable* practice to tease those who are visibly not like the status quo?

Eight powerful authors have chosen to share short stories of school bullying in relation to children with special needs. Each author has experienced the trauma often associated with school bullying through the lens of a parent and/or educator, which is often painful to speak about and write about. These eight authors share their painful stories in hopes that their experiences will shed light as to the mental, emotional, financial, and physical tolls bullying has on families of children with special needs. It is the hope of our authors that as you read through these intimate stories, you, too, will join in the fight to eradicate school bullying of *all* children—especially those with special needs.

# CONTENTS

| | |
|---|---|
| Title Page | iii |
| Foreword | 1 |
| Introduction | 5 |
| 1. She Looks Normal to Me | 11 |
| 2. The Day Bullying Visited My Home | 21 |
| 3. Black Males with Disabilities Bullied by a System Not Designed to Protect Them | 29 |
| 4. The Fractured Pieces of Bullying | 39 |
| 5. Bullying Hurts . . . Period | 49 |
| 6. Layers of Life | 59 |
| 7. Bullying: A Family Spectrum | 69 |
| 8. The Parent-Principal Partnership | 75 |
| 9. Your Thoughts | 85 |
| Personal Reflections | 87 |
| How Can I Help Prevent Bullying? | 93 |
| Final Thoughts | 99 |
| About the Author | 101 |
| Connect with the Author | 103 |
| Leave a Review | 105 |
| References | 107 |

*Chapter One*

# SHE LOOKS NORMAL TO ME

## By Ann Bernardi, LCSW

After trying to get, and stay, pregnant for years, Jane was the baby of my dreams. We knew, however, that she was different from the beginning. She was extremely fussy, spending most of her time in my arms, either nursing or screaming. She was intolerant of textures, both on her skin and with regard to her food, and she had a hard time connecting with others. Once her little sister was born, it became even more apparent that, while she looked normal, there was something that made her exceptional.

As she got older, we had daily struggles with behavioral issues, meltdowns, rigidity, and aggression toward her younger sister and me. This occurred especially when trying to get her to do something she didn't want to do, which was pretty much everything. She was obsessed with certain things—fixations and restricted interests that took up a great deal of our time and attention. When she turned four, I decided to take her to Children's Hospital in Richmond for an evaluation. She was difficult from birth, but her behaviors were escalating and I was exhausted.

I'll never forget the day I met with the psychologist and she gave me the results of her testing on my daughter. As she delivered her diagnosis, I felt a rush of relief, and at the same time, the terrifying realization that this was not going to go away. The psychologist seemed a little flippant in the way she spoke. "The long and short of it is that she is twice exceptional. She has a very high IQ and Asperger's syndrome. Good luck." I grabbed the evaluation and my daughter's hand to leave and then remembered that this was not a child you could just grab and take out of her current situation. I sighed deeply, bent over, and explained to my daughter that it was time to go and that I was going to give her five minutes to complete what she was working on and then we would need to leave. I geared up for an epic battle. The psychologist and I just stared at each other awkwardly, and she reminded me that she hadn't finished reading her evaluation and recommendations to me. I reminded her that I, too, had a degree and could read it myself. In hindsight, I may have missed some important information, but my mind was reeling and I felt the need to flee. Her last comment to me was about how beautiful my daughter was and how this was going to be a double-edged sword for her. I could swear she was giggling when I had to physically remove my screaming child from her office.

Immediately, I made up my mind that I had work to do and an action plan to put in place. As I began my research, I realized that I myself had a distorted idea of what Asperger's looked like. Even as a mental health professional, I was uneducated and up until that time, I had only known males who had that diagnosis. As I learned about Asperger's and neurodiversity in general, I mapped out some things on which to focus with my daughter. Social skills training and emotional regulation—specifically how to manage the anxiety in dealing with social situations—were at the top of my list. We put Jane in occupational therapy, and I spent time daily swinging her, brushing her, and desensitizing her to various textures and foods. Every day we practiced speaking to others, making eye contact (or faking it), shaking hands, answering teachers, and learning basic social skills, like not picking up a book in the middle of playing with a friend and saying she was done. It was exhausting, but once I saw a little bit of progress, I was determined to keep it up for as long as needed.

I made the decision to keep my daughter out of public school during her early elementary years. She attended a Montessori program that was perfect for her, but at the end of her second-grade year, she announced she was ready for a "real school" and that she wanted a "big school experience." I attempted to get her to stay the course and then transition into high school, but she was insistent and focused on moving to a public school. I didn't think she was ready for the social experience, and I was afraid she would be picked on by those who didn't "get" her. She was often complimented on how pretty and smart she was, and many still didn't understand when she acted oddly. By this time, she knew of her diagnosis and didn't want it to be common knowledge. She acknowledged that she knew it would be a change but assured me she was ready for it.

I met with the principal who looked at her work portfolio

and suggested she be placed in fifth grade. I explained to him that while she had been allowed to advance academically in Montessori school, she wasn't ready emotionally or socially to be in a class with all fifth-grade children and face the reality of middle school the following year. I gave him the psychological evaluation and explained her diagnoses, but he just shrugged and said, "She looks normal to me." This certainly wasn't the first time I had heard this exact phrase. It was often followed by, "I would have never known" or "She doesn't seem like she has Asperger's." I wondered how much my helping Jane to be more superficially neurotypical was actually harming her. Reluctantly, I signed her up for public school and somehow, she connected with the nicest girl who loved Jane, despite her eccentricities and the challenges of being friends with her. No matter how poorly she behaved, this girl dragged Jane around with her and made her part of the popular group of girls and boys.

However, inside, Jane was struggling. She felt like an imposter and was constantly on edge. Navigating the social scene in public school was really hard and she was bored academically throughout her three years of elementary school. The academics improved in middle school, as she was put in more advanced classes; but she continued to struggle socially. She camouflaged as best as she could and tried to fly under the radar. She had some friends and had grown comfortable with them if things were going well. I did my best to explain her quirks and idiosyncrasies to her teachers. Several said that they could see the Asperger's, but many more just expressed how surprised they were by this diagnosis, as she "looked normal to them."

I questioned her diagnosis myself, but everything I had read about Asperger's in females really seemed to fit. The behavioral and neuroimaging findings in research seemed to suggest that autism manifests itself differently in girls. The criteria for autism spectrum disorders are based on data that is derived from studies almost entirely of boys. She didn't look like a typical child with Asperger's because clinicians are missing girls who have this less disabling type of autism, and we haven't seen them in the numbers that we have seen for boys.

I told Jane that I wanted her to play a sport to try something new and branch out. She tried out for field hockey and to her horror, she made the team. She was awkward and clumsy and had almost no skill. Holding the stick and dribbling were torture, but she hung in there and ended up playing throughout high school too. She really wanted to participate in the school's Odyssey of the Mind (OM) competition, so my friend and I signed up to be the coaches for the team. We quickly got a team together and immediately I knew there was going to be trouble between my daughter and one particular girl on the team (we will call her Katie). The other children, boys and girls, reported back to my friend and me that Katie was being mean to Jane. She was making ugly faces at her, rolling her eyes when she spoke, and consistently telling her that her ideas were stupid. Katie continually did this while saying it wasn't just her opinion, but that she had done OM in the past so she knew what they should be doing. She was much more adept socially and loved to perform, sing, and act. Jane hated the idea of performing and decided that she was a "backstage" person. I noticed her staying away from Katie as much as she could and I watched her shut down creatively. The team was tasked with creating something and making a presentation, but my daughter continued to withdraw from the process.

I didn't realize it at the time, but the children on the team later told me that Katie went out of her way to be mean to Jane. She would wait until my friend and I were out of earshot and say something negative, passive aggressive, or downright rude. We attempted several times to catch her, but she was very adept and sneaky. When confronted, she just smiled and said it wasn't true and that the other team members were just picking on her. Things changed when the team was all sitting together one day, and the other coach and I were in an adjoining room with a sliding glass in between that had been left open. We were organizing handouts to go home, and we heard Katie say clearly, "I don't like you, Jane. I don't like you one bit." I could see Jane from where I was standing, and I saw her sad face turn to anger as she finally stood up for herself. "How can you not like me? You don't even really know me?"

The girl answered, "I know enough to know that I don't like you."

Jane responded, "Well, if you don't like me for no reason, I guess I don't like you either because that's not nice or fair or smart." At this point, their voices were raised and the other team members were telling Katie that she had been mean to Jane for the last two months and that she needed to stop.

Her mom pulled up outside, and she ran out of the building and got into the car. The damage had been done, though, and Jane didn't intend to back down anymore.

For the rest of the time together, we attempted to keep the girls apart and overall the group worked well when supervised. They did so well, in fact, that they placed at the regional tournament and moved onto the state championship. While we had downtime in between our competition and the final ceremony, our team and the parents decided to spend some time at a local park. The children wandered off to a stage to hang out without us. Suddenly, there was a scream and then crying. We all rushed over, and Katie was holding her leg and crying. She blurted out that Jane had kicked her and that her leg was hurt. Jane did martial arts and had participated in the Junior Olympics for Tae Kwon Do so I was legitimately worried that she may have hurt her. Without giving her the benefit of the doubt, I yelled at her and told her to go sit in the car. She tried several times to speak to me, but I was embarrassed and refused to listen. After Katie had calmed down, the other children got together and approached me. They related that Katie had been picking on Jane, calling her names and implying that she was retarded. They said that when the other children stuck up for Jane, Katie became enraged and attempted to attack her physically. Jane was able to block her and then kicked her hard in self-defense.

I felt horrible. Worst-mom-ever moment. Here my child had again been the victim but wasn't sophisticated enough to look like it. The other coach approached Katie's mom, but backed off when she heard the narrative taking place between the parents and the child. It was obvious that they were not interested in the truth or correcting their own child's behavior. They had laid the blame on Jane and were labeling her a bully. I decided to just get through that day and reached out to the school to ensure the girls would not be in class together. We went to the state championship, and I kept a tight rein on Jane, protecting her from the subtle but very damaging bullying that had come to be the norm from Katie. She loved to sit and stare at Jane while she spoke, smirking and rolling her eyes. Any attempt to correct her was met with denial and further claims of victimization, though none of the adults or children ever saw any bullying from Jane toward Katie.

I knew that we wouldn't make any progress with the parents, and I realized how deep the issue was when I was working as a PTA member at the talent show. I had asked Jane to bring my youngest daughter backstage to me if she started to cry. I could hear my baby crying but couldn't figure out why she wasn't bringing her to me. She later told me that she tried to get back to me, but that Katie's mom had stopped her and told her she wasn't allowed, even when Jane explained the situation and that she would return to the audience immediately. While I appreciated the attempt to keep the girls apart, it would have taken less time and energy to simply have walked my daughters back to me as I worked backstage. I was furious and grateful that the girls were moving on to high school where there was almost no chance of being in the same classes.

Fast-forward to junior year when surprisingly they were in the same class. Jane came home and told me she couldn't believe that Katie was still picking on her. According to Jane, Katie had told the entire class about a girl (Jane) who had previously attacked her physically. Just like years earlier, she liked to stare at Jane. She did this when Jane was speaking to the class, or Jane would catch her randomly staring at her and making faces. Katie enlisted the help of a friend to be more verbally aggressive toward her and continued her snide comments under her breath, her eyes rolling whenever Jane spoke. I offered to have her moved out of the class, but Jane had been fortified and said she didn't care because Katie was irrelevant to her.

Jane said, "Katie is sad and jealous and most people don't like her."

The more I listened, the more I realized that Jane wasn't going to fall for the BS any longer. In fact, Jane told me, "I don't want to be someone who is mean."

My heart shattered into a thousand pieces as I listened to Jane's rationalization behind not retaliating against Katie after her comment to the entire class. My daughter confided in me that she thought Katie might have the same type of diagnosis and that she had clearly not benefitted from treatment right from the start. What a mature response from a teenager!

I was beyond proud that she had gotten to a point where she neither needed to fight back nor internalize the other person's dislike for her. She had empathy and insight, and there was some recognition of herself as the special human she was. Still, I spoke to the school counselor and he doubted me. In fact, he said, "It would be weird that Katie would bully

Jane, as there usually is a power differential and as far as I can tell, Jane has more power."

I immediately pushed back. "The difference in power is due to her Asperger's."

He then had the audacity to further question my daughter's disability. I could tell he wasn't buying it and as I got up to leave, I heard him say, "She looks normal to me." I confronted him about his statement.

In my mind, I was pissed off—his comment was rude and out of place. While keeping my professional composure, I told him in a calm yet firm tone, "Thinking that children who have a diagnosis on the spectrum and all 'look' a certain way is detrimental to them as a group, and individually." After taking a deep breath to calm myself, I finished with, "Having treatment for years has helped her to fit in better."

As a counselor, he needed to understand that underlying dynamics and challenges still existed for my child. While I realized that improving her ability to socialize and fit in may have hurt her in this particular situation, it had helped her immensely. She did look normal, normal for her, and I couldn't be happier.

## Chapter Two
# THE DAY BULLYING VISITED MY HOME
### Florence Spencer, DBA

Going to school is about learning and building relationships, but that's not the case with children who are different or perceived as different. They are subjected to some of the most mean-spirited behavior that most school administrators and parents would not believe. It has been argued that children don't understand how their words can affect someone, but I disagree. Once a child gets a reaction from their words—good or bad—they understand how powerful that word(s) can be. Incorporating how words can hurt should be a conversation that starts at home by the parents and not after an incident has taken place in school. Children with special needs didn't ask to be born with these afflictions and deserve to learn in a peaceful and safe environment just like children who are perceived as "normal."

If I were asked to describe someone with special needs in two words, it would be *strong* and *loving*. Regardless of the curveballs life has thrown their way, these children always seem to have a smile on their faces. My son had Duchenne muscular dystrophy, which is a terminal disease, and up until the day he died, my son never once complained, nor did he let his illness get in the way of him living the best life he could possibly live. However, he did have some roadblocks appear along the way—not just with his health but also with school. He once made the statement that going to school was not always a pleasant place to be.

The first time we came face-to-face with bullying was during my son's freshmen year of high school. He was very excited to enter high school, and I was very excited that he was healthy enough to still attend school. Everything was going well at first; he was happy and always talked about how his day went and his new friends. However, that seemed to change right before Christmas break. He was not being very vocal about his day and his enthusiasm about attending school was slowly diminishing. I just assumed he had settled in and was being a typical teenager who really doesn't want to share with his parent. During the Christmas break, that fervent spirit had seemed to return. He was engaging and wanted to talk about everything. It was like he had a weight attached to his wheelchair and someone took them off so he could maneuver better. When the break was over, the night before returning to school, my son said something that made my blood run cold: "I don't want to go back to school because this boy is so mean to me and makes fun of me."

The different waves of emotions I felt were so hard to

describe. As a mother, I wanted to kick myself for not noticing or questioning the change in his behavior. There was a part of me that wanted to transfer him to a new school, but I knew there could be a chance of this happening again. Then, I wanted to cry my eyes out because of what he was going through. That night, we talked about some of the things that this boy had done and said to him. We also talked about who he alerted to the issues he was having with this child. His answers made me angry because this child was bullying several students. The only action that was taken by the administration was moving the child to another class. What was even more alarming to me is that I never received notification from the school of what was going on with my son or the action(s) that was taken to alleviate the issue.

According to my son, moving the student only made it worse because he would wait in the halls to taunt him, kick his wheelchair, slap his food on the floor during lunch, and demand that my son purchase *his* lunch. At that point, I had heard enough and made the promise to my son that I would rectify the situation. He didn't want me to take any actions because he didn't want to look like a snitch. However, I reassured him that he would not look like a snitch—he would be a hero for coming forward and helping the other students who were being bullied by this young man.

It was a restless night for me; I tossed and turned all night thinking about what my son must be feeling. Moreover, what incident this young man experienced to cause him to become a bully. The next morning, I took my son to school and went to have a conversation with the vice principal or the principal. I sat in the waiting area looking at all the children rushing to class, and it made me wonder what percentage of students were being bullied with no one being the wiser. Just thinking about the students who were too afraid to tell anymore made me sick to my stomach. I couldn't (and tried not to) imagine what was going through their minds having to come to school every day to face this living hell.

After ten minutes of waiting, the vice principal greeted me and directed me to her office. When I told her the reason I was there, she was a little taken aback that I would make the trip all the way to the school to talk about this and not just send an email. Her words were like plunging into an icy lake. Therefore, I took a few minutes to get over the shock before responding. Gathering my composure, I told the vice principal that this was a serious matter and sending an email was not sufficient. Then I peppered her with questions as to why I was not notified when this issue was first brought to their attention and when it was resolved. Immediately, I was met with, "It was an isolated incident and was handled swiftly."

Calmly, I asked, "How do you know this was an isolated incident? Don't you think the parents should be made aware of any matters that pertain to their child?" The question was never answered; I, in turn, asked for a meeting with the principal and my son's teacher. I thanked the vice principal for her time and excused myself. As I left the school, tears streamed down my face. I wanted to scream, I was livid. Moreover, it felt like my blood was boiling in my body.

That afternoon, I received an email from the principal apologizing for the ongoing issues my son was having and granted me a meeting with her and the teacher that coming Friday. I was surprised by the email because the principal's words indicated that my son was still being bullied. This was in contrast to what the vice principal had told me—that it was an isolated incident. When my son got home, I asked him about his day and he said it went well because the young man did not attend school that day. He also said the principal came to his class and talked to his teacher. In addition, she went to two other classes and spoke with those teachers as well.

Friday took forever to come, and the more I tried to keep my mind off what was going on with my son and how poorly it was handled, the more it became harder to focus. I wanted to protect my son from this child. Most importantly, get reassurance from the school administration that if an incident like this is brought to their attention, they would immediately investigate and reach out to the parents. In addition to investigating, there should also be a follow-up process to ensure that the matter has not resurfaced.

Friday finally arrived and as I sat in the waiting area, I noticed there was another parent there waiting as well. The principal came in and greeted the both of us; apparently, the principal reached out to the young man's mother after sending me the email. It did make me wonder about what communication procedure the school followed when reaching out to parents. Nevertheless, it was a welcomed opportunity for everyone to sit down and figure out what needed to be done to stop the bullying. The child's mother didn't look too happy to be in this meeting and once we sat down, I soon found out why. Seemingly, this young man was in trouble often and this was one of his many infractions. My son's teacher spoke first and listed the documented times that she had to remove this young man from her class before he was transferred to another class. The child's current teacher then spoke and again, there was a laundry list of issues she was having with this child as well. This child was unruly; prior to this meeting, the child was reprimanded for taunting another student in the class. This was very disconcerting to me because there were no real consequences for his actions. Finally, the mother spoke and insisted that her child was the one being bullied. The mother took no responsibility during the meeting. I felt that we had not resolved the matter.

When it was my turn to speak, I expressed how displaced I was by how this matter was being handled. Not only was this an ongoing matter, but it also appeared to be taken lightly. My son was being bullied for months, and it was taking a toll on him. He was not the chipper child I was used to seeing. He would get so nervous and sad every morning before going to school and if this was his behavior at home, I could only imagine how withdrawn he was in school. I stressed how this was detrimental to his school performance and most importantly to his health. Dealing with muscular dystrophy was already a burden on him—and now he was being bullied every day. This was too much for my child or any child to handle. My heart ached for what he was going through.

Feeling the frustration building within me again, I took a

deep breath to calm myself down. Once the frustration had subsided, I made it clear that I wanted a resolution to the matter or I would take other actions, such as going to the school district to file a complaint and even taking my concerns to the media. The principal could sense the frustration and quickly chimed in. With understanding in her voice, she asked what I would like the process to be going forward. Directing my words toward the teachers and principal, I demanded that parents be notified via email, letter, and phone when an issue such as this arises. Also, I suggested that bullying should be addressed in PTA meetings and during training and development for teachers. There should be some type of training for the teachers on how to identify and handle bullying in their classroom. I didn't address the mother of the young man because I felt that it would have led to a debate over whose child was bullied and whose wasn't. However, the mother agreed with my suggestions.

In the end, the school did make changes in how they handled bullying. Parents were notified when an incident occurred and the school invited guest speakers to talk to the students about bullying. Teachers were also trained on how to identify and handle bullying in their classrooms. My son slowly reverted back to his happy, upbeat self again. As for the young man, I never received a follow-up on how the matter was handled and I never saw the child or his parent at any PTA meetings.

Experiencing bullying firsthand opened my eyes to how it can play a big role in a child's behavior and the decisions they make. My son was lucky that the administration was willing to hear my concerns and stepped up to make changes. However, there are millions of children being bullied every day. Bullying is scary, and the outcome of bullying is even scarier. What's so sad about this issue is parents and school administrators are sometimes unaware of what's happening. Moreover, by the time they are made aware of the situation, it is too late.

*Chapter Three*

# BLACK MALES WITH DISABILITIES BULLIED BY A SYSTEM NOT DESIGNED TO PROTECT THEM

By Benita Kluttz-Drye, MSW, MSA

The Individuals with Disabilities Education Act (IDEA) mandates a free and appropriate education for students with disabilities, yet black students identified with disabilities face many challenges. They are tasked with maneuvering and matriculating through an educational system that was not designed with them[7][8] or their academic successes in mind.[9][10] Moreover, black students who receive special education services are misclassified for placement[11] and are disproportionately referred for special education services as compared to their white peers.[12] In fact, black boys only make up 10 percent of students in public schools yet equate to 18 percent of those classified with a disability.[13]

Black males identified with disabilities receive more frequent and harsher disciplinary actions[14] for more minor infractions than their nondisabled, white counterparts[15] and are 11 percent more likely to be in schools where law enforcement officers are present.[16] They have bleak and despondent labels placed upon them. These labels are often detrimental,[17] create social isolation, dehumanize them,[18] and carry stigmas,[19] indicating little hope[20] or an ability to be successful academically or otherwise.[21]

Stigma and fear of black males, with or without disabilities, are often heightened by the media[22] and "African-American boys know all too well what it feels like to be viewed as a 'problem' in schools."[23] The criminalization of black males further exacerbates the problem[24] because society demoralizes and identifies black males as being savages, dangerous, and aggressive beings, embodying no moral or ethical notion.[25,26,27]

When we think of students with disabilities being bullied, we imagine the bullying being perpetrated by other students. However, current research supports that black males with disabilities are often bullied by the educational system charged with teaching them.[28,29,30] This is evident in how these students are treated, addressed, or ignored in schools by teachers, administrators, and school staff.[31] Examples of mistreatment include being labeled as "bad,"[32] encountering subjective disciplinary actions,[33] and having teachers embody a deficit stance rather than a strengths-based approach.[34]

For this chapter, *bullying* is defined as an exertion of power or force through actions, laws, policies, responses, or behaviors that result in others feeling powerless, victimized, dehumanized, or helpless to advocate on their own behalf.

In this chapter, I will focus on how the infrastructure of special education can perpetuate acts of bullying. I will explore the impact of implicit bias, disciplinary disparities, and stigmas associated with being classified as "special ed." All of these are forms of bullying often experienced by black males who have been identified with disabilities. Specifically, this chapter will discuss how educators responsible for teaching black males with disabilities can also be the ones perpetuating acts of bullying and violence against these students.

This chapter will also examine this crisis using the *deficit thinking theory* by Kenya Walker.[35] Deficit thinking theory suggests that students identified with disabilities and their families are the problem[36] and are the blame for students' academic failures, lack of involvement, or behavior issues.[37] Deficit thinking theory further suggests that these students are incapable, incompetent, and unintelligent.[38] Educators who embrace a deficit-thinking stance believe that black students have limited abilities or opportunities to be successful because of their culture or background.[39] These educators often take a position of colorblindness and do not believe that it is necessary to consider students' culture when developing curriculum and instruction.

As both a special education teacher and a parent of a child identified with a disability, I have witnessed and advocated against such injustices. I have also seen students identified with disabilities be hindered by a system that is supposed to support, develop, and promote access to resources and opportunities. However, this has not always been the case. The system has failed and committed acts of bullying against black students identified with disabilities.[40][41][42]

One example of bullying is through the deficit approach that the system has created to afford access for students identified with disabilities. Specifically, the educational system is designed to identify students as being the problem or as having a problem before they can receive needed support.[43] According to IDEA, students must be identified with a disability and this disability must be impeding their learning or academic success before they can be provided with certain guarantees or assurances by law. Students needing additional help and support are often not provided support without first being classified with a disability.[44] Typically, classrooms are not designed or set up to provide students with automatic support. The constant focus on testing and linking a teacher's performance rating to how well their students do on tests have created an environment where teachers are more focused on getting students ready for testing rather than spending time enjoying the teaching and learning process.[45] In essence, teachers do not have the additional time in their schedule to provide modifications and/or accommodations unless mandated to do so. Moreover, many of these classrooms do not consider or incorporate differentiated instruction or Universal Design for Learning or consider the various modalities of how students learn best or support needed to be successful.[46]

In 2016, we moved to a new state for new opportunities, or so we thought. When my son first entered his new school, he was met with a system that did not provide him with the support he needed to do well in school. Gavin (pseudonym), who is currently an eleventh grader, was diagnosed with ADHD, color blindness, and dysgraphia since he was in the third grade. As a parent and fellow special education teacher, I have always met with the schools and worked with his teachers to create the support necessary for his success without the need for an official Individual Education Plan (IEP) or services under Section 504 of the Americans with Disabilities Act. He had always done well taking advanced classes, and regularly made the honor roll with this support. The accommodations included the ability to record his notes or receive copies and to receive extended time on test and homework assignments. However, when we moved to a northern state during his tenth-grade year, we found some stark differences in how things were done. Although Gavin had these needs, he had never had a formal IEP or been served under Section 504, which would require that he received the needed support. His teachers had always worked with us to incorporate accommodations and differentiated instructional strategies that allowed him to be successful. They freely and willingly provided extra time on tests and homework and paired him with a peer for notes.

During his first-quarter marking period in the new school, we noticed he was struggling to keep up with everything. He was often up until after midnight regularly completing homework and he was failing most of his tests even though he knew the information. When I asked Gavin what was going on, he told me that he often didn't have time to complete the tests in class and that his teachers would not give him extra time to complete them despite my having previously talked to them. In fact, Gavin stated that when he asked his teacher for additional time to complete his test, his teacher said, "If I give you extra time, it will be unfair to the other students. You just need to study more." Gavin reported that this made him feel "slow" and "stupid."

As a result, I contacted the counselor in writing and requested a meeting to discuss putting a 504 plan in place. It was clear that accommodations were not going to be done freely or willingly. As a former special education administrator responsible for compliance issues regarding IDEA, I am well aware of my rights, safeguards, and due process. However, the counselor advised me that the referral would need to come from the teacher. She also met with my son after the written request and told him that he needed to change his classes from honors classes to general classes. It was clear that the school did not want to go through the process of meeting, creating a plan, or providing modifications and accommodations.

We were continually met with delays and stall tactics four weeks after my written request. It was only after I advised the school of my experience as a special education administrator, cited due process regulations and statutes violation, and that I was pursuing a PhD in special education did anything change. Once they realized I did indeed know my rights, they apologized and there was a morph in their attitudes and behaviors. Everyone became overly helpful. They even offered to provide Gavin with extra time without an IEP or 504 plan.

However, I declined and informed them that I could not trust that they would do what was in my son's best interest without legally being required to do so. It was very disheartening that my son, as an eleventh grader, had to be classified for special education services before he would be afforded with accommodations necessary for his success. As a parent, my heart also goes out to other parents who may have faced similar situations but were probably unaware of their rights.

This was a clear instance of the system attempting to bully me and my son through the special education process.

Special education teachers should be champions and cheerleaders for their students. They should not be the ones who deflate students' confidences. When I was a special education teacher, many of my students came into class feeling defeated and incapable, embracing learned helplessness, and carrying labels placed on them by the school system and society. These students had experienced many years of failed attempts, low expectations, and limitations placed on them by teachers who told them they were "incapable" or "stupid" and that they would not be successful in life.

This learned helplessness resulted in students believing that they were not as smart and could not be successful, resulting in no motivations for trying. My greatest successes as a special education teacher came through building relationships with my students, demonstrating a warm demeanor, and holding high expectations for them. I would not allow them to say, "I can't," but rather, "I will try," and "I can do it!" Unfortunately, these attributes aren't embraced by all teachers. Many teachers view students with disabilities from a deficit mind-set and embody tenets of implicit bias.[47] Implicit bias is "the unconscious biases that people are unaware they hold but influence their perceptions, behaviors, and decision-making."[48] Implicit bias reinforces subjective discipline referrals based on race and results in disciplinary disparities.[49] Black students are 3.8 percent more likely to be suspended than their white counterparts.[50]

Education should be a gateway to future success. However,

extreme discipline policies, such as zero tolerance[51][52] coupled with a deficit and implicit bias mentality,[53] does not garner a safe, productive, learning environment for these students. Rather, black males with disabilities, especially those classified with high-stigmatized disabilities, such as emotional and/or behavioral disturbance or mental retardation,[54] are "more likely to be subjected to intense school control than white students."[55] Frequent discipline referrals also result in students being viewed as bad or troubled students. Black boys with disabilities who have frequent suspensions face a double jeopardy.[56] In addition, teachers who embrace deficit thinking, display implicit biases, or who buy into stereotypes of black boys are more likely to make quicker discipline referrals for more minor infractions.[57] Moreover, the way black boys with disabilities are treated is influenced by their discipline record. Students who have an extensive discipline profile are more likely to be viewed as "bad" and treated according to how they are perceived.[58]

Gavin has never had a discipline infraction in his academic career. However, he was perceived as defiant and disobedient based on his race and his physical stature. He had been in his new school for fewer than two weeks. On this particular day, he left home wearing a baseball cap. On the way to school, I asked him if they could wear caps. He stated they could and proceeded to tell me of students in his class, who all happened to be white, who frequently wore hats at school. Later that day, I received a call from the school and was advised that my son was in the office for refusing to remove his cap and that I had been called because they knew that my son "was one of the good ones." I advised the school that I was on my way at that very moment to discuss the matter. I met with my son and the assistant principal and asked what happened. The assistant principal said that they were at lunch and the lunch monitor, who I later learned was a white female, had asked my son to remove his hat and that he had refused. I turned to my son and said, "Gavin, I'm surprised. This doesn't sound like you."

He said, "Mom, she didn't tell me to remove my hat. She said, 'Do you want to remove your hat?' and I said, 'No ma'am. I'll keep it on'." This situation illustrated the cultural misalignment or lack of cultural synchronization[59] between white teachers and the black students they teach.

*The examples expressed in this chapter are just a few of the situations I have observed as both a special education teacher and a parent of a child with a disability.* There is still much work to be done. There are also several implications as a result of these experiences. Teachers should have professional development and continual implicit bias training to examine how their individual thoughts and perceptions shape their responses. In addition, teachers should become well-informed of and use culturally responsive teaching to help their diverse learners connect to what is being taught. Finally, schools should promote Universal Design for Learning. Students should not have to be referred for special education services for accommodations that can take place in the classroom through good teaching practices.

*Chapter Four*

# THE FRACTURED PIECES OF BULLYING

## By April J. Lisbon, EdD

As a parent of children who have been bullied in schools, I am frustrated with the number of children who are unable to ride the school bus, sit in their classrooms, play on the playground, or even eat in the cafeteria in fear that they will be picked on in school.

Enough is enough.

Everywhere you turn, especially in the news, stories about cases of bullying seem never-ending. For example, I can recall a story back in 2017 about a parent recording her child's bully to "prove" that indeed the bullying behavior was ongoing. The parent had had enough and more than likely felt that the school was not taking her child's case seriously, as the bullying continued. Unfortunately, in her state, her recording was deemed a criminal offense. In this particular case, it was illegal to infringe on the privacy of others without their consent even when you, as a parent, know that the bully is causing harm to your child. In some school districts, if the victim gets into a fight with the bully, both can be arrested even if your child is acting in self-defense.

As we are all aware, bullying of *any* kind is *serious*. The number of children who are bullied at school and on social media is rising every year. Yet, parents, educators, and children may not be fully aware that in many states, the type of offense may lead to criminal charges. You read that correctly: criminal charges with severe penalties.

I know this from personal experience. One of my own children was the victim of bullying. In his particular case, the taunting and teasing were not the offense. Instead, the act of asking for money in exchange for *not* assaulting my child was the offense.

Do you remember hearing about bullies asking children for their lunch money in exchange for not beating them up? Were you the victim? Were you the bully? No matter the role, exchanging money for "protection" has serious consequences. It's considered extortion.

Extortion? That's correct. In the state where we resided, once my child gave the bully the money for "protection," it became a criminal offense. I knew this prior to heading to our local sheriff's office with my child as I researched this type of offense on the internet. However, like many parents and as an educator, I had no idea what this would have meant for my child or the bully.

Let me set the stage for you, the reader:

*There were four boys at the bus stop who seemed to get along at one point on their school journey. But one day, one of the boys decided to tease the other boy in front of his peers. The other boy asked the teaser and his friends to leave him alone. Now let's fast-forward a few days later when the teaser told the victim that he would not beat him up if he gave him money the next day. Problem? Absolutely, as the child paid the bully not to harm him. However, the results were nothing that the victim's family or the bully's family would have ever predicted.*

This happened to my child. In speaking with the deputy on duty, I learned that this exchange in our state was considered strong-armed robbery. *Strong-armed robbery?* When I initially heard those three words, I was scared. My heart began racing, my eyes were widened, and I was in utter disbelief. If I could scream and swear simultaneously, I would have. For crying out loud, we were talking about middle schoolers. What the hell? They were the same as my child. Besides, when I consider strong-armed robbery, I always associate it with a weapon being used.

As I pondered it more, I realized something immediately: there *was* a weapon. It was the bully's mouth and the words that made this a crime when he asked for money in exchange for my child's safety. As a parent, it became more real to me when another deputy further explained that in our state, the punishment would be up to twenty years in jail.

Wow!

Think about this for a second. An eight-, eleven-, or thirteen-year-old could spend all their childhood and some of their adult years in jail. Now imagine what this would mean for the victim. First, the victim has to relive the bullying event as though it were happening to them once again. Next, if the victim decides to prosecute the bully, their peers might view them as a snitch. No one wants to be considered a snitch, especially in secondary education. Unfortunately, there aren't any real winners in these types of situations, as both the victim and the bully have paid prices, which is unwanted emotional turmoil.

Reliving the trauma of bullying is a gut-wrenching experience for the victim and their families. At any point in time, anyone or anything may trigger the unwanted emotional turmoil(s).

I had hoped this would not be the case for my child, but it was. Unfortunately, this time, the bullying created a space where my child no longer wanted to be physically present on earth. My child was assaulted on the school bus one day by a "friend." Initially, he was reluctant to share the event with me. However, he did, and I was proud of him. Like any parent, I followed up with the appropriate school personnel and it was found that indeed my child was assaulted.

As his parent, I was excited that this time around, the bully was caught and the school believed my child. When I shared this moment with my son, he appeared to be happy that the issue would be resolved.

Everything that seems to be okay is not always okay. After I shared the results with him, my child was not himself within an hour after hearing the news. Being that this student rode the same school bus as the previous students discussed earlier in this chapter, the idea of riding the school bus and going back to school the following day must have consumed him mentally and emotionally. Why? Because at that point, my child went into a dark place and wanted to die. My middle schooler wanted to die because he didn't want to face the next day. Compile that with the autism, and it was a complete implosion.

I had no other choice but to save my child's life. I had to get the appropriate community professionals involved so my child would live to see another day. Yes, he may not have liked my decision at that moment, but my job as his mother was to protect him physically, mentally, emotionally, and spiritually.

Has this ever happened to you? Have you been in a place where you have had to call community professionals to help save your child's life? How did it make you feel? How did it make your child(ren) feel?

To hear your child engage in thoughts of suicidal ideations or attempt to harm himself in your presence is truly debilitating. My heart wept for my child because he is a brilliant and amazing person. He always smiles and makes others feel like they belong. Yet because of some of the "quirky" behaviors often associated with autistic children, his neurotypical peers may not always make him feel like he is one of them. We all want to belong and feel wanted. Bullying takes this away from children!

As I said before, to hear your child state that life was no

longer worth living is a debilitating experience. Due to the ongoing bullying, there was a point on our life's journey when my child was hospitalized. During this process, I experienced firsthand the limited support and services available for individuals with autism. To know that an autism diagnosis minimizes a person's chances of receiving mental health support in our society was jaw-dropping. Are you kidding me? Regardless of what side of the vaccine debate you are on when it comes to the *cause* of autism, just know that depending on your location, finding a hospital bed will be hard no matter how old they are based on my personal experience. *Prepare, prepare, prepare.* I wasn't prepared for such an event to occur within our family. I wished that I had made sure that I had enough financial and emotional cushion to help me and my son during this crisis. I hope this never happens again. However, if it does, I'm already creating a plan.

Throughout this process of bullying that my child experienced during his seventh-grade year, I felt ill-equipped to support his needs even as a school psychologist. I felt like nothing I said or did was helping this situation. I was broken emotionally, because this was my baby and it seemed like our lives were spiraling out of control. I felt like we had done everything right, but the results were not what I anticipated. Like many parents of children who have been bullied, I needed someone to tell me what I should do if my child were bullied.

So, what can you do as a parent?

First, carefully read up on your state's laws regarding

bullying so you have a clear understanding of what this could/will mean for your child if s/he is the victim, bystander, or bully. Knowledge is power, so the more you know, the more empowered you will become if your child ever faces such an issue.

Second, *report, report, report*. It is not enough to report this issue to your child's principal or school, as I learned in our case. Once the offense has occurred, the offense should be immediately reported to the school resource officer (SRO). If there is not an SRO at your child's school, report it to your local law enforcement agency once you are aware of the issue. I followed protocol and alerted the school with no response the first time. After I witnessed the exchange of money between my child and the bully, I alerted the school again. I had no clue that this should have been reported to the SRO or the local sheriff's office until I shared my story with those on social media. Once I was told to report the issue to the local authorities, my child and I went to our local law enforcement agency the next day.

Third, praise your child for sharing with you their concerns about being bullied. In our case, my child was not the type who would say that he was being bullied, as he didn't want me to think differently of him. He made it seem like all was well and that the children were friends again. It was not until I told my child my own personal story of being bullied that the truth came out. My child was afraid that if he told me what had happened, his bully would beat him up. He was even more afraid to share it with local law enforcement, as he was unsure what would happen to him if he shared his story. I reminded my child that he was doing a good thing (all children have a right to go to school safely) and that bullying was not acceptable by any stretch of the means. By praising my son and allowing him to share his story with both our local law enforcement agency and the SRO, my child felt empowered that something would be done.

Fourth, connect with your child's school to learn if bullying workshops for parents are being offered. If not, ask them to offer them at the beginning of the school year and at the end of the school year. It's great to have conversations about bullying at the school level with students; however, I really doubt if many of the videos and bullying curricula accurately address the legal ramifications that may occur if one engages in an act that is considered a criminal offense in one's state. With these workshops, I would highly recommend that school teams copresent these trainings with their local law enforcement agencies so schools and parents have a clearer understanding of how law enforcement agencies not only view these offenses, but also how they would prosecute such cases.

Fifth, I know that it can be emotionally and mentally draining to learn that your child is being bullied. I initially felt helpless in my situation. I felt like the school wasn't doing anything to hear my cry for help. There was a moment in time when I wanted to confront the bully's parents after the money exchange. However, depending on how the conversation was perceived, I may have looked like the aggressor in the situation. Why? It was my word against theirs. When you're working on high emotions, you have no idea what you may say or do in such a situation. This may not be a good move on your part depending on your state's laws when it comes to engaging in confrontational situations surrounding issues related to bullying.

Sixth, depending on your child's special needs, it's important that you're aware there will be limited resources and services to care for your child when you need it most. I learned this the hard way. Working paycheck to paycheck or having employee insurance may not cover the cost to care for your child. Prepare today for what may happen tomorrow. Never in a million years would I have ever imagined that my child would be hospitalized. The estimated cost to cover his stay was astounding. This didn't include the ER bill, staying at the local hospital, or the ambulance that was used to transport him to a more specialized hospital. Find ways to create additional streams of income so that caring for your child(ren) is no longer an obstacle. This experience was my best teacher. Why? Because I've learned to only attract those opportunities where I am of service to others, especially when it comes to saving for crises.

Finally, as parents, we must understand our state laws with regards to school bullying. Regardless if you are the parent of the child who is the victim, bystander, or bully, there are many consequences for *your* child's actions that will create emotional turmoil for everyone That's why I'm encouraging you, the reader, to take time out to really understand how to protect your child and yourself if ever faced with bullying issues. Too many children have lost their lives to bullying. Don't allow your child to be one of the statistics. According to Moon and

Alarid, "Prevalence estimates range from 20 percent of students reported being physically bullied to 50 percent of students reported being verbally or socially harassed." Let's cover our children with special needs and work together in the fight to stop school bullying.

## Chapter Five
# BULLYING HURTS...PERIOD
### By Magalie A. Pinney, BA

Bullying is when one child or a group of children repeatedly pick on another child who is weaker, smaller, and more vulnerable. In recent months, I have learned about different and real-life instances where physical size had *not* played a factor.

Penelope attended a reputable charter school. She enjoyed her education and social encounters as an elementary student. Upon entering middle school, things began to drastically change. A group of peers would taunt, tease, and ridicule her. Penelope was a healthy-sized girl of good stature. The bullies were made up of other girls. She was not timid. She spoke her mind and expressed herself to her teachers and peers alike. However, when she brought it to the attention of both her parents and the school administrators, she was left to fend for herself against the accounts of the girls who outnumbered her. She was even accused of making up details, and her parents were informed of the same. Her parents didn't see the need to question the school, so they took the school's and girls' sides instead of their own daughter's. The occurrences increased and worsened. The once-secure, bold, and expressive Penelope had, over time, become frail emotionally and mentally. She eventually attempted suicide. Her parents' eyes were brutally awakened.

Darren excelled in his academics and sports activities and was bright and talented in several areas. Yet when he witnessed a child of one race name-calling and pushing around another child of a different race, he couldn't keep silent about what he had seen. The child who was being attacked had tried to calm the situation and back out, but the bullying child was relentless, so he was left with no choice but to fight back and fight off the bully's aggression. This led to school administrators penalizing both children. Darren, being a child of mixed races, told his mother how he wondered what would have happened to the kid who fought back if he had been the same race as the bully. He was a middle schooler who had never had to question fairness at his school up until that day.

Bullies try to control others with scare tactics, manipulation, and intimidation. He/she wants to be in charge to improve his/her own esteem. She seeks attention she may be lacking at home where she can receive it at school, on the school bus, or in the neighborhood. He is hyper-aggressive, and his victims are initially meek or become meek over time.

When I researched bullying and learned what it was, what it consisted of, and to what extremes it can affect other people's children and their families, I breathed sighs of relief that my children and family had not been affected firsthand.

We have restricted our kids' use of technical devices to include phones, computers, and tablets so that they are used in common areas only. We have established technical security monitoring to block them from being sought in this manner and to prevent them from seeking out others in this manner.

But regularly practicing these measures does not make our children immune. Bullying is a pervasive phenomenon that cannot be controlled online or offline.

I learned this with two of my three children with the odds being against their favors two to one. My earliest foresight into the possibility that my younger daughter, Vivian, was being bullied was when she was three years old. My husband and I had picked up our children after working at their private Christian preschool, which was predominantly serving families of color. During pickup, a teacher had approached me to discuss the days' worth of activities. I had looked away and observed two other little toddlers seemingly playing with my daughter at one of the play table areas of the center. The two girls were taunting and teasing my daughter for smiling and laughing at what they had made fun of her about. My child was actually going along and laughing with them as if she did not understand that she was the initial focus of their laughter. That made my heart sink in sadness because her demeanor had always been happy, eager, friendly, and social, but she was my nice girl. I had no control over her not-so-nice little playmates.

I didn't address it then and there with the teacher or my husband because I was honestly shocked and surprised children so young could start behaving in alienating, superior manners. Yet that was my telltale sign. I didn't think that my daughter's teachers would allow things to get out of hand if behaviors like this fell under their radar.

By the first grade, Vivian was in love with her new school, her new friends, and her new varied, diverse, socioeconomic environment. She had joined her older sister at this public elementary school. Her younger brother was in kindergarten there as well. By all accounts from my open house and parent-teacher conference meeting held with her young teacher, Vivian was a stellar student with her strengths being math, reading, and class participation.

By winter, her potty attentiveness had regressed. She was bedwetting. She was sneaking extra food into her backpack. She preferred to stay home than to go out on our regular outings. When she did go on outings and playdates, she became anxious to return home. She whined repeatedly and complained when things didn't go the way she had wanted. She became moody, angry, and withdrawn.

During the last week of December just before her school's winter break, my daughter informed me that a classmate of hers had asked, "You know you're ugly, right?" This first grader told her this in the classroom to her face. Wow! I gave her three chances to self-advocate during the first week of January by simply going to her beloved teacher to tell her what had happened. Vivian conveniently forgot to bring it up after each time I had asked her about it. So, I told her that if *she* wouldn't speak up and stand up for herself by telling a trusted adult, *I* would have to go to her school and advocate as soon as I could get there.

I went to her school's office and waited to speak with an administrator. The assistant principal met me and walked me to his office to discuss the manner. I told him everything I had been told by my daughter and I was firm with the severity of this instance even though it involved first graders. The seeds had been planted firmly for my child.

He didn't want me to be present. He assured me he would address this. He arranged with both her teacher and the other child to take both children out of their classroom so he could speak with them, one-on-one, in a separate room about this matter. I followed up with my daughter, who was embarrassed about this confrontation. She wouldn't stand up for herself. She didn't think of herself as important enough to defend her own worth and beauty. She had the right to be able to learn what she loved to learn in school without being name-called in such a mean, upsetting way.

The name-calling hurt me because it had hurt her, but it wasn't surprising to me by then that this could happen to her for looking like she does or for being different from another person in a mixed, racially diverse setting such as this new school. I was thankful she had at least come to a trusted adult with this information—me, her first advocate and her first teacher. I was grateful for my child's honesty. I was pleased she realized how she had been treated was wrong. By now, she was aware that being teased and taunted was not right at all.

She had also confided to me about a separate classmate who was taking her snack, but it was because she was hungry. Vivian was bringing her extra snacks from our home because her friend's parents were poor and struggling. Heartbreaking for me, but coming from the other end of the emotional spectrum. From that point on, I had her pack two snacks for them both the next week. She kept a snack for herself and gave the other snack to her friend. The moral is this: beauty is not only in the physical eye of the beholder—it is entrenched within the heart of the teacher and the student as well. She still had her heart, and her compassionate and friendly demeanor had remained intact.

But boys are very different than girls. Several years later, my daughters are now attending a different school than my son, Nathaniel. They are in middle school, and my son is in fifth grade. He had suffered from many bouts with social anxiety and general anxiety since he was a preschooler, though not while he was in his school setting. These instances almost always occurred when he was in unfamiliar, new settings with new people and new children. He feared the unknown and unexpected routines. These fears impacted his being able to remain calm and friendly with other children. He suffered from separation anxiety whenever I was not nearby or in the same room with him.

As years passed and he became older, these instances were fewer and farther between, for which I was both thankful and grateful. I was pleased that he had been able to overcome some of his anxieties on his own, but one method that would've helped to alleviate or circumvent these instances is if I had opportunities to introduce him to his new environment ahead of time. I would've appreciated orientations, screenings, and open-house events.

Nathaniel's father had been picking him up from his bus

stop after school. They came home one afternoon to inform me there had been a series of events occurring on the bus and at school. On the bus, older kids were bullying the younger kids for seats in the farthest back ends of the bus. Several of these boys and girls had continued fighting after reaching their shared bus stop. The bus driver wasn't stopping these incidents. They had been addressed by administration afterward in school. Future instances would lead to student suspensions and/or expulsions.

At the school, there had been roughhousing during recess time between my son and his classmate. According to my son, both boys were just play-wrestling, but they wound up losing both their glasses—they fell off and only one of the boy's glasses broke. Both boys were brought inside and taken into the assistant principal's office. Both of their actions were addressed with both being found to be equally at fault. Both boys agreed that this would not happen again and that the other boy's glasses would need to be replaced by his parents, not us. Both boys returned to class and that would be the end of the matter.

However, the issue escalated, because rumors began to spread among the students in their class and from other classes about what had happened since the incident. The other boy's parents were not pleased at having to pay for their son's glasses, so they were coercing their son into influencing my son to get us to pay for the cost to replace the glasses instead. During lunchtime and recess time, cliques formed where the kids began to sit at separate tables, one being my son's and the other being the other boy's. Random kids, male and female, would ask either boy what they were going to do to resolve the matter themselves.

In effect, these kids were looking for both boys to fight about this after school. These suggestions and threats had lasted a few weeks before Nathaniel informed his father and me.

The stress and anxiety of the confrontations about the bus incidents, the accident in play at the school, and the intervention by the teachers and assistant principal proved to be too much for my son to continue to bear silently. He had already lost his friend and he had grown to accept that this was one result. Yet, had things not intensified with the larger group of students, would Nathaniel have even confided to us at all? Why was this left between the two boys and his parents? Why were both of us not informed directly of the matter? Apparently, one of us had been initially (my husband), but being that boys will be boys, he had figured that this would be a one-off incident with the handling of the matter at school.

Bullying and cliques being formed as a result are nothing new, but they seem to have intensified since my generation was in school. Not only has it continued to occur on campus, but also it is now happening online and via text and emails. Our youngsters are now killing themselves over these issues. There used to be times when most kids would just accept their low to high social rankings in schools and keep pressing on. They were more willing to accept that not everyone is likable and not everyone is accepted and we cannot force these things either way. Now adversity can easily push so many children over the edge.

The precipitating factors themselves can be trivial, accidental, and serious. As parents, we chose to keep the lines of communication with our son open. We followed up with him regularly regarding his bus and school experiences. We listened to his feedback. Based on this communication, we planned to follow up directly with his school personnel and administration should anything have intensified physically or verbally. Our son didn't want to have any confrontation. He didn't want to have to speak on any part of the matter with his peers. But what he thought had been squashed had been resurrected by the other boy's parents, which resulted in a whirlwind of other behaviors and expectancies by the other children. The children act older than they should. The adults act younger than they should.

A child can become a victim of a male or female bully or a group of bullies. I attended a Families First Parenting Program workshop where I discovered the warning signs for parents and guardians to watch for in your child or children. Learn from my story and watch the warning signs! Their future depends on it.

*Chapter Six*

# LAYERS OF LIFE

### By Keisha Jennings-Samuels, MAE

**H**ave you ever closed your eyes and dreamed that the world was full of laughter, hope, and prosperity? You settle in on your dream, which is filled with the pursuit of happiness, and then a dark cloud starts to tiptoe in your direction. As you see a massive, dark cloud approaching, you try to run away as fast as you can. At that point, you realize the dream you had is now stacked with sadness and there is no way out.

That dream turned into a reality once I sent my autistic son to school.

In 2007, I gave birth to a baby boy, the apple of my eye. When he was born, I vowed I would never let anyone or anything harm him. As he started to get older, I noticed he wasn't developing like other little boys his age. I knew that something wasn't right, because I have worked with children on the autism spectrum and with children who have an emotional behavior disorder. A few days went by, and I made an appointment with our family practitioner. He referred my son to various doctors because other medical issues were also prominent. At my son's gastrointestinal appointment, the doctor noticed that he wasn't functioning mentally like kids his age, so he referred us to the Marcus Autism Center. I called the number given and scheduled an appointment. It was after several days of testing that my son was given a diagnosis of autism.

At that moment, I could think only of the challenges that my students in the special education classroom had to deal with daily, such as bullying from their peers in the general education classroom. Now my child would have to face bullying issues and try to survive in a world that does not understand autism. As I sat and pondered about all the challenges my child would receive from his peers, I reflected back to what I told him when he was a baby: *I will never, ever let anything or anyone harm you.*

As days turned into weeks and weeks turned into months, I became lost. I was no longer just an educator who worked with kids who had autism. I was now a mother with a child on the autism spectrum, and I was hurting. I was no longer a vibrant pearl in the ocean. I was a drifter walking in a lifeless body. At that moment, my son and I were no longer mother and son or parent and child. We were thrown into a world where prejudice, hate, and misinformation were given about individuals diagnosed with autism. As the years went by, my son's temperament changed, his preferred clothing and food options changed, and the world around him changed. How could I help him? I didn't have all the answers, but I did have the option to protect and advocate for my son in this world when his voice was silent.

What a joyous day it was when I received the news that my son could begin school at the age of three and a half years old. I wasn't sure if I wanted him to go, but I saw how successful he was when the therapist from Babies Can't Wait came to work with him. This was another chapter in our book of *I Told You So* to all the doctors who said my son would never be able to do various things like ride a bike. Looking back at it now, they made me want to fight for my son even more and prove them wrong. I shook the Magic 8-Ball and asked if the doctors were right. The Magic 8-Ball answer was a little cloudy that day. But what if the Magic 8-Ball had the capability to tell me what was going to happen to my son as he aged? I could save him from things that were destined to cause him harm. However, the Magic 8-Ball could not provide that service. I had to walk through this journey with determination and love.

At three and a half years old, my son started attending a special education preschool program at the local elementary school. It was during this time that I started to learn about the world of special education as a parent with a child who has special needs. Even though I worked in the school system, I was now put into a position where I was no longer sitting at the IEP meeting as an employee of the school system; I was a parent being thrust into a situation that I could not control, or at least not to a certain point. My son attended this school until he was in first grade, and then our family moved to a new school district. This was when our journey with bullying began and my trust in the education system started to deplete.

At the beginning of my son's first-grade school year in 2015, I felt that things were going to be different. I heard from several neighbors within my new community that this particular school was one of the best schools in the county. I was told they had an excellent principal, but I feel the usage of the word *excellent* is often determined by the individual's perspective of that person. My son's first-grade teacher was wonderful, nice, and pleasant. She was the impeccable picture of what a teacher should be. During that time, my son loved to go to school; then one day, he became overly aggressive. Yes, he had meltdowns at times, which was just a part of his personality. However, the behavior that he was displaying was not typical of him.

Every day for two months, I asked my son how his day was at school and he would look at me with the meanest look on his face. His eyes were squinted, his nostrils flared, and he no longer gave me a smile. His fingers were glued to the palm of his hand as his arms rolled up to touch the sky. Before he could try to hit me, I protested that "when we are mad, we calm down and take deep breaths—we do not hit anyone and we use our words." Though the words came dripping out of my mouth like a running faucet, they seemed to evaporate once within reach of my son's ears. We would go on to have this conversation frequently. As his behavior kept changing, I contacted his teacher and asked her if he was displaying a negative behavior at school. His general education teacher and special education teacher told me he was doing well at school and they didn't see a behavior change in him. Though I was given this information, in my heart I knew something wasn't right.

Therefore, one day after school, I decided to change the way I asked him about his day. I channeled my inner psychologist. I sat down next to him with a bag of gummy bears and started telling him stories about my experiences in school. Between every second and third statement I made, I would say, "You know you can tell Mommy anything even if it's bad."

To my surprise, he started asking me questions about how I handled situations at school when someone was being mean. I said, "First, I told my mom when someone was being mean to me." Suddenly, the lightbulb went off and tears started running down his face. He looked at me, but he did not utter a word. I told him that it was okay, and I asked him if he wanted to draw a picture of what was going on. He nodded. I handed him a piece of paper and instead of him drawing a picture, he wrote the word *throw*. I looked at him puzzled and said, "Throw?" Then I asked, "Is someone throwing something at you?" He nodded. I asked him, "Who is throwing something at you?" He wrote the child's name on the paper. I hugged him and told him everything would be okay.

The next day, I spoke with his teacher and showed her what he wrote. As the teacher looked at the paper, she said, "I'm sorry." She hugged me, she cried, and she stated that she didn't know. That day, I thought it was going to be the last time my son would have to deal with bullying.

Another school year had emerged; it was the 2015–2016 school year. My son was in second grade. We started the year talking about bullying and what he should do if he encountered a bully or witnessed someone else being bullied. The school year started off well, and he made one friend. Then one day, he started to display negative behavior. Once again, this was not the typical behavior he would display when he was mad. He was displaying the same negative behavior in the past when he was being bullied. His nostrils were flared, his eyes were squinted, and his fingers were glued to the palm of his hand. At that moment, I knew something was not right. I reluctantly asked him every day to tell me what was going on in school. My son and I would have the same conversation for several weeks. I went up to the school and spoke with his new general education teacher and his old special education teacher. I told them that my son was displaying negative behavior and I believed something was going on at school. Both teachers told me that nothing was happening and that he never came to them with a problem. When I heard these words again from his special education teacher (who knew what happened last year), I tried to stay calm, so I smiled and walked away. I told myself I would start my own investigation.

I had the same conversation with my son about my childhood experience in elementary school. This time, when he wrote on paper, the word *throw* was not there. But at that moment, I wished it were. The words *knife* and *kill* were written on the paper. I gave him a hug, then rushed off to speak to my husband about the matter at hand.

After speaking to my husband, I went to my computer and wrote to his teachers about what was going on. I told them that I needed to speak with them and an administrator as soon as possible. When I arrived to drop off my son at school, I immediately went to the teacher to see if she received my email. She informed me that she had not read any emails that morning. I asked her if I could speak to her in the hallway and I told her what was going on and who the student was that made this threat to my son. Her eyes opened wide and her mouth dropped. Then she said, "I know what student you're referring to, and he has been causing lots of problems in my classroom." She also stated that she would contact the principal about the matter.

Then I proceeded to walk to the special education teacher's room. Like the regular classroom teacher, I asked him the same question, "Did you get a chance to read your email?"

He looked at me and said, "I already contacted the principal about the matter." Over the next thirty minutes or more, we spoke about what my son told me. There was, however, one question that the special education teacher asked me that upset me: "How come your son didn't say something sooner?"

I immediately replied, "My son does not know how to communicate when someone is being mean to him. He does not understand facial expressions or verbal expressions that people use in a negative context." Then I turned around, grabbed my son's hand, and walked away. He was no longer going to attend a school where this was happening until the school fixed the problem.

After about three days, the special education teacher and I spoke about the matter. Again, I was told that the principal was contacted and that she had steps she had to take. Therefore, I contacted the principal and I never received a response from her, which shocked me. I kept wondering why the principal was not responding to my emails or calls.

As days went by, my son missed more days of school because I didn't want him to go back into an unresolved situation. Finally, I received a call from the special education teacher who updated me on the progress. During our conversation, he asked me if I wanted to put my son in a new classroom. At that moment, I removed the phone from my ear and stared at it for a minute; then I put it back to my ear. I told him, "Let me speak with my husband before giving you an answer." When I hung up the phone, I screamed at the top of my lungs, "Why would you want to remove a child who has a hard time with transitioning and being in new environments into another classroom? He is not the problem—he is the victim! Why would they keep the child who made the threats in the classroom? Why would they keep a child who has been having behavioral problems in the classroom? Why not move *him*?"

After calming down, I spoke with my husband and he looked at me and said, "Are they serious? No!" At that very moment, I sent an email to the special education teacher, general education teacher, and the principal that my husband and I did *not* want our son to be moved to a different classroom. I also stated I wanted to have an emergency meeting.

The next day, a meeting was to be held between the principal, the general education teacher, the special education teacher, and me. Once I arrived at the meeting, the principal didn't show up. I was told that she had to attend another meeting. I tried to stay calm, but it didn't work. I requested that I wanted another meeting by tomorrow and an administrator needed to be there.

The next day, we had another meeting. The third- and fifth-grade vice principal attended the meeting. During the meeting, I learned that she was unaware of the situation because she was not the vice principal for my son's grade level. At that moment, she was updated on what had been happening. After she learned what was going on, she said, "Your son should've said something sooner. Bullying is not allowed at this school."

I pushed my chair away from the table and slowly looked at each person in the room. I said, "This is not just a bullying matter. This is classified as terroristic threats according to the school handbook and school policy. I do not want the little boy who made these threats to be charged with a terroristic threat because he is only a child. However, something needs to be done and if something happens to my child, I will sue this school."

I walked out of the meeting.

A few days later, I received a phone call from my son's special education teacher and he told me that the principal was going to take care of the matter. I was happy to hear that the matter was going to be resolved, but I was still disappointed because the principal and other administrators did not reach out to me personally. Days later, I took my son back to school and spoke with the classroom teacher. She told me that the child who made the threats was suspended for a few days, but she was unsure if he was going to come back to her classroom.

Then it happened: the little boy was back in the classroom.

As I walked my son into class, I made eye contact with the little boy. He stared at me, then put his head down on his desk. The teacher walked over to me and informed me that the principal was not going to move the little boy to another class. However, my son's desk was moved closer to her desk and the little boy was told not to interact with my son. She also stated that she would keep an eye out for my son.

At that moment, I was in shock because I couldn't believe that the school and the school system had failed my child. I allowed my son to stay in the classroom, which is a decision I often ponder about daily. However, I became an avid volunteer in my son's classroom until the last day of school. My voice was not heard by the school administration, but my son heard the voice of his mother's love and determination to fight for his rights.

*Chapter Seven*

# BULLYING: A FAMILY SPECTRUM

### By Sharon O'Malley, EdD

I would like to preface this chapter with some background information about how I came into this arena. I am sharing some of my personal thoughts and observations about my son, Robbie (pseudonym), who was born in 1990, following an easy and uneventful pregnancy. Robbie was the second of our four children. By the time Robbie was two years old, my husband and I knew he was quite different from our older son, born four years to the day before his little brother. After two more years of visits to numerous specialists, we received a diagnosis of Asperger's syndrome. When the neurologist went on to explain, I felt the room spin. I was at the bottom of a well, his words muted before me. So many questions were running through my head. I replayed two years of consultations and speculation.

*Well, it's not autism, right? It's not autism, right? What's wrong with him? Oh, he's just a terrible two; oh, he's just a middle child. Now he has this thing called Asperger's syndrome. What? It's autism. Autism? I'm just going to jump out of your window right now. I'm going to jump right out of the window. I head to the window and see I'm on the ground floor. Sucks. This sucks. I am numb. I put him in the back of my car in his car seat and I drive home. I drive all the way home and I look at his little face in the car seat and I look at what we have ahead of us. I hear one of his teachers saying, "He might work an assembly line."*

Twenty-three years have passed since that day, and I still don't know how this story will end. As is sometimes the case, children with autism can also develop mental health issues. In my son's case, it was anxiety disorder, obsessive compulsive disorder, and later, bipolar disorder and depression.

Having not heard of this syndrome before, we started to research what we could do. Our son was now in kindergarten and was suspended more than once for behavioral issues in the first month of school. The district was unaccommodating and viewed my husband and me as adversaries. I began to look closely at other public school districts in our area and started calling them. I learned that some of the districts that had remarkable state test scores and graduation rates didn't consider the special education students. They were sent to other districts. This was in the mid-1990s where school choice options were limited, and the internet was only beginning to emerge as a strong research and communication tool.

We moved our family to the exurbs of the city, hoping to

find the best fit for each of the unique learning styles and special needs of our children. That meant moving away from our urban neighborhood and putting our children in a suburban public school system. While we only moved ten miles away, it was a completely different world and our family missed being able to walk to the library, grocery store, and school. I felt disconnected from the community, but moving was our only choice. I don't regret that decision, as it was the best option available at the time.

Robbie felt marginalized from the time we moved to the new school. Frankly, he never fit all the check-off boxes to identify any specific disorder neatly. The autism spectrum box offered a chance for early intervention and was a close enough fit. He had an attendant who helped make sure he got on the correct bus, had his supplies, and offered amazing support to help him be prepared to learn.

Our son still resents us for imposing this support and adamantly believes that he was branded at school and treated badly by other students because everyone thought there was something "wrong" with him. There is no question that my son was bullied in school. Bullying takes many shapes and forms. At its most blatant, bullying serves to denigrate the victim and fuel the bullies. It can also take on a much more insidious format. It is a subtle sense of being unwelcome. He was never invited to a birthday party. He couldn't understand why his siblings had playdates and invitations, but not him. Even now, the thought of that still breaks my heart.

The district did a very comprehensive job in preparing my

son for academic achievement. His teachers worked as part of a meaningful team that included us. They appreciated his aptitude for difficult subject matter and his sense of humor and creativity. Even so, we could have done better. Though academically prepared, he was not ready the first time he tried to attend college, having not learned the life skills most do from observation and intuition.

Looking back and speaking to Robbie now, I believe there are many very doable things that can happen inside the schools to support students who are isolated and feel ostracized by their peers. Lunchtime can be one of the most miserable. Robbie told us how students would move away when he sat at the table. Perhaps implementing a rotating seat assignment would benefit lonely students as well as the popular ones. Teachers need to pay attention to the social growth of their students and find ways to curtail hurtful practices such as distributing party invitations in front of those students who were not invited.

Life skills and basic living skills—balancing a bank account, learning how to cook and budget—should be taught both at home and at school, and tested in school like any other subject. My son is brilliant but also naïve and at risk for becoming a target of an unscrupulous landlord or salesperson. Those are some of the things that others absorb almost by osmosis. Other children, like my son, miss the nuances and often lack insight into what others are thinking and what their motivations might be.

Our family was fortunate in that we were able to relocate to a superb public school district that never hesitated to provide services and support. Once Robbie graduated high school, though, he fell into a crevice, having aged out on some options. We were left to manage on our own. There remains a lack of coordination between school and social service providers that might offer innovative solutions to the unique issues facing these children.

Having a special needs child is a very isolating experience—the entire family is affected. Other students identified my other children as Robbie's sibling. They also felt labeled and stigmatized but have since moved forward to become successful and happy in their chosen careers. For a very short time, we enrolled them in a program for siblings of those with autism. Sadly, the program disbanded, leaving little support outside of our family for the other children. While they were very social and had many friends, there was no longer a place where they felt safe to express their anger and frustration with their brother.

I'm at a point in my own life where I feel like I can finally catch my breath and begin to ask, *Where do we go from here?* My own children are grown now. Robbie is living back at home with us, taking some college courses and looking for his own apartment. I am confident he will be fine as we push him out of the nest and into the adult world.

No singular person can effect change alone. As a mother, I will continue to be the grizzly mamma advocating for all of my children, even now that they are grown. As educators, we have a duty to ensure that our students also learn about empathy, compassion, kindness, and how to help others thrive. My child entered the public education system on the cusp of the autism boom in the early 1990s. Whether or not there is an actual increase in autism cases or just increased awareness about how it presents itself remains to be seen. Regardless, it is time to make some very practical improvements about how students on the spectrum are provided with the emotional support necessary to thrive after high school.

*Chapter Eight*

# THE PARENT-PRINCIPAL PARTNERSHIP

### Raphael Crawford, EdD

My journey from frustrated family member to advocate-leader began with having a nephew who was developmentally delayed and non-verbal during the first years of his life. I watched him struggle for acceptance, dignity, and respect. . . and to be included in the routine activities and games other children played. I observed his love for riding a school bus to an environment that was, at best, apathetic and ill-prepared to meet his specific needs. When he was physically beaten by staff at a "special school" for children with exceptionalities, I experienced an inept response from the principal. I have advocated, confronted, and threatened legal recourse against the schools that failed him; but I felt defeated. I have watched in angst while people in public places sometimes stared, laughed, sneered, or became offended when he reached out to hug them; and I was often brought to tears.

Like families of other children living with exceptionalities, mine has experienced the feelings of embarrassment, guilt, pain, and hopelessness. We made the decision to pull him from public school and educate him at home, which took dedication and great effort. With an amazingly strong mother and sister, and my network of my personal friends who are educators and healthcare professionals, my nephew learned to speak and to perform many basic self-care activities. Because I had personally experienced life with a child who lives with challenges and so that I could better advocate for and address the needs of other students like him, I went back to school to earn a graduate degree in special education. I switched from teaching science and literacy to teaching special education. I knew that the education system of which I was a part did not value special education students and only marginally satisfied the requirements of the IEP. I still believe this to be true today.

The role of the school principal has changed significantly and has become a high-pressure bureaucratic position that hinges on high-stakes test results and the ability to successfully maneuver through competing and often poorly implemented mandates and requirements. As such, principals may be even less likely to give the required attention to students with exceptionalities that they deserve. My experience as a special education teacher and as a successful elementary and middle school principal, along with my personal experience with a family member who lives with exceptionalities, have shaped my practice and advice to parents and school administrators. I advise parents to look for, and principals to focus on, action, advocacy, and expectations.

**Action**. The single most important thing a principal can

do for families of children living with exceptionalities is to give them a voice. Parents must know their worth and understand the power in their voice. The principal must empower these parents by ensuring that they fully understand special education laws and local school district policies related to special education services. An informed parent is much better positioned to advocate for their child, and this is a responsibility of the principal. It should be the principal's sincere desire to be accessible, compassionate, and empathetic. Parents of children living with exceptionalities don't want sympathy or special accommodations; they want realistic and compassionate solutions, and they want schools to provide the best possible services and educational experiences for their children.

The principal must humanize children living with exceptionalities and insist that everyone else in the learning community does the same. These children and their families deserve the same dignity, respect, and opportunity afforded to everyone else in the school. Know their names and call them by name! Make them feel valued, respected, and wanted!

When school personnel greets students they encounter but ignore special education students they pass, this is a significant red flag and indicator of the environmental norms—address it immediately, as courtesy and kindness should never be withheld based on the perceived presence of an exceptionality. The principal who is willing to simply listen and show a little human kindness, and then commit to resolving issues, becomes a valuable partner with the child's family.

The principal who is truly committed to providing exemplary services to students living with exceptionalities articulates and demonstrates this in his or her leadership beliefs and practices. Actionable indicators that parents should look for in a principal include:

• Advocates consistently for the student and family; fights for improvements to services; speaks publicly for laws that protect and support special education students and their families;

• Advances knowledge of special education laws and related school district policies; ensures that special education laws are followed and that the school fully complies; takes ownership for ensuring that parents fully understand special education laws;

• Commits to providing exemplary special education services; ensures an inclusive educational experience; takes ownership of ensuring instructional and socialization goals are met; sets the tone for the provision of special education services in the school, as well as for providing a safe and supportive environment for students and their families;

• Participates in IEP and 504 meetings, actual participation, not simply signing documents; ensures that IEP and 504 plans have clearly written steps for monitoring success and progressive steps for transition; and

• Values children over costs; provides education services that are truly in the best interests of the individual child; ensures that services are child-centered not cost-prohibited.

The principal's ability to recite common special education terminology does not indicate any level of proficiency or advanced knowledge of special education. Principal preparation programs generally do not include any instruction on special education, and unless the principal was a former special education teacher, he or she is likely deficient in this area. I suggest that parents ask their school principal for school-based learning opportunities for families and staff, as this would provide great collaborative learning and partnership-building.

**Advocacy.** The principal who is sincere about providing exemplary special education services and supporting students and families automatically becomes an advocate, without apology or fear. That principal also empowers parents to advocate for their children and themselves. Great principals develop leadership skills in others. As previously mentioned, giving voice to parents is the greatest tool of empowerment in getting needed services for children with exceptionalities. Nothing gets attention from a principal or superintendent like a direct email or certified letter from a parent or group of parents with a concern or compliment.

When the child enters a new school, or has a new principal or teacher, I strongly suggest that parents request in writing a meeting with the principal, teacher, school counselor, and any other person who will serve the child. This allows the family and school staff to discuss and understand the unique needs of the student, as well as expectations from the family, and sets the tone for building a positive partnership. This is not an IEP or 504 meeting and should not be treated as such. While principals wear many hats, this meeting is one he or she should attend rather than send a representative.

Critically important is teaching children with exceptionalities how to advocate and speak for themselves as they are able.

Often, adults fail to acknowledge the feelings and desires of children with special needs; these children deserve to be heard and to make their choice known, even non-verbal students must be taught how to make their choices known and to advocate for themselves. In the school setting, it is the principal who is accountable for ensuring this skill is taught to students with exceptionalities. The principal is also responsible for ensuring that students and their families know what resources are available and that they have easy accessibility to those resources.

Part of teaching advocacy skills to students and families is teaching what to advocate for, as well as how and where to seek help and resolution to concerns. Principals must monitor the advocacy skills of students and families and ensure that they are empowered to speak for themselves.

**Expectation**. The school principal sets the tone for the school and all things related. Parents must look for, and the principal must clearly articulate, an expectation of acceptance, inclusion, and safety for all students and their families. All staff, students, and families must know and understand the expectations for the learning community; this must be a nonnegotiable for the principal. The principal must humanize students with exceptionalities and normalize their complete and full inclusion in the learning community, ensuring that they are included in every possible aspect of the school culture.

While parents are responsible for making the principal and school aware of their child's unique needs and the things that help with an optimum learning experience for the child, the principal is accountable for normalizing acceptance of and appreciation for individual differences within the community of learners. Students living with exceptionalities should never be invisible! The principal must never allow adults—school or district staff, visitors, or parents—to disregard, disrespect, or minimize special education students (or any student) in any way. Every school employee must be empowered to intervene and redirect the poor behavior of the adult visitor. Students living with exceptionalities are part of the fabric of the school, and are the responsibility of every school employee, not just special education staff.

Principals are duly obligated to provide a safe and secure learning environment free from threatening and disruptive behaviors and activities. Therefore, the principal must continually work toward maintaining a safe and respectful experience for children living with exceptionalities and their families. These children must be made to feel safe with the principal.

Unfortunately, bullying is prevalent in both schools and general society; no child or student is likely to escape at least some degree of bullying. Principals cannot realistically guarantee that students will not experience bullying; however, they can declare and commit to their campus being a "Bully-Free" or "Safe Zone." Protecting children living with exceptionalities and maintaining a safe and responsive learning environment is critically important. Schools are responsible for earning the confidence and trust of parents of these, and all, children; parents must be reasonably assured that these vulnerable children will be protected while in school.

Because many children living with exceptionalities cannot clearly articulate specific details of bullying, the principal must ensure that there is a "safety plan" in place to monitor and supervise these children while at school or when participating in school-related activities. Likewise, the entire school staff should receive professional development related to special education laws, student safety, and principal expectations for provision of special education services. Nonverbal students and others who appear defenseless are sometimes prime targets for bullies. Schools must work with families of these children to understand specific gestures and ways in which the children communicate feelings, especially their discomfort. It is essential that principals and school personnel understand the difference between manifestation of a condition and reaction to a situation; children are further traumatized by isolation and punishment because they could not articulate their anxiety and frustration about an offense.

Children living with exceptionalities must be taught how to communicate choices, desires, and feelings to staff; incredibly important is the schools' obligation to ensure that these children know from whom to seek help in the learning community. If possible, these students should be taught how and when to communicate "no," "help," and "stop."

The principal must clearly articulate that no bullying will be allowed at the school. Often, parents of children receiving special education services are bullied, treated disrespectfully, or ignored. I suggest that principals immediately address this unacceptable and unprofessional behavior; it must never be allowed to happen. The principal must ensure that all people on the school campus receive dignified and respectful services always. Principals and school staffs must work to ensure that theirs is a culture that accepts and embraces individual differences.

Placement in special education programming must never be a barrier to being included in the school community. Children living with exceptionalities have many of the same interests as their peers and are eager to participate but are often not considered—this exclusion must not be allowed to continue. The principal must make sure that his or her staff understands the expectation to create opportunities for children living with exceptionalities to participate in school groups and activities. Likewise, the principal must work with parents to put them at ease about allowing these children to participate because, in most cases, parents have grown accustomed to their children being excluded.

During my years as a school principal, I required coaches to add children living with exceptionalities to school teams and clubs, and it almost always was appreciated and received well by the coaches. Seeing the excitement in the faces of these children, included with their peers and wearing a team uniform, was only second to the excitement and pride displayed by their families; I always knew that it was the right thing for the students and school. Additionally, I included these children in honors awards ceremonies, reciting the morning pledge, pep clubs, cheerleading, and many other student activities. Schools have an obligation to build the socialization skills of all students in an inclusive learning environment. The principal—as advocate and school leader—must ensure full inclusion in the school's general program.

There are no "magic bullets" for making inclusion work for

all students and in every school; however, it is the principal who drives the culture of the learning environment. The principal must be an ardent supporter of children living with exceptionalities and their families. The principal must accept the role of defender and protector of these children and be committed to improving educational services for them. The ability to love and support students who may not be able to positively add to the school's achievement scores is a strong characteristic of this advocate leader. Ensuring the success of children living with exceptionalities is the binding goal upon which the parent-principal partnership grows.

## Chapter Nine
# YOUR THOUGHTS

We, as the authors, would like to thank you for reading our short stories of school bullying in relation to our children with special needs. Everything cannot be captured in one book, as sometimes reliving one or more moments of bullying can and will elicit the trauma to be experienced once again.

Honestly, our journeys have been tough, and daily we will fight to ensure that *our* children lead productive and happy lives for as long as they can. However, we cannot fight this journey on our own. We need *your* help!

This section is divided into two parts. The first section will afford you the ability to share your thoughts and feelings as to what you might have learned about school bullying and individuals with special needs. The second section will allow you to think through how you can join with us in our fight to eradicate school bullying for children with special needs.

A few pages have been added to help you write down your ideas. You may choose to use less, more, or the number of pages that have been provided in this book. Be inspired—what you write down may change your life or someone else's.

## PERSONAL REFLECTIONS

Date: _____
_____
_____
_____
_____
_____
_____
_____
_____
_____
_____
_____
_____
_____
_____
_____
_____
_____
_____
_____

# HOW CAN I HELP PREVENT BULLYING?

Date: _____

_____
_____
_____
_____
_____
_____
_____
_____
_____
_____
_____
_____
_____
_____
_____
_____
_____
_____
_____
_____

# FINAL THOUGHTS

Bullying continues to be a serious issue in our society, especially in schools. As parents and educators, we may question if our schools and/or local school districts have established adequate policies to address bullying, given the increase of violence and deaths associated with bullying from year to year. We may even question if they are doing or have done enough to protect children who have been bullied both on and off school property. We must move beyond questions and start hearing real answers!

Each author provided the reader with a small glimpse into their lived experiences of school bullying in relation to children with special needs. With raw emotions, every author expressed the highs and lows of the lasting effects of school bullying on these children. Yet in the end, each parent and/or educator continually advocated for their child or children's needs so that the cycle of bullying would not continue.

Not one more child should contemplate death or actually die by the *hands* of school bullying! *Enough is enough.*

Therefore, it is important that law enforcement agencies and school districts work hand in hand with parents to help address the issue of bullying, as it's not going away any time soon. It's not enough to have bullying posters hung up in school buildings or have "conversations" about bullying after watching a video on the issue. No! As a collective group, we must understand what our state laws say about bullying so that we as parents understand what this could mean for the bully, bystander, or victim not only in the present moment but also in the future. There will be cases where schools will indicate that the victim's case was unfounded.

If you as a parent still have concerns, mediation with district-level personnel and/or legal counsel may be appropriate. We're talking about *your* child. We must put an end to school bullying for *all* children. They are our future.

# ABOUT THE AUTHOR

April J. Lisbon, EdD has worked tirelessly to advocate for the needs of children. She has learned that it is challenging raising children with exceptional needs. She is the author of *Stretched Thin: Finding Balance Working and Parenting Children with Special Needs, Autism in April: A Mother's Journey During the Tween Years,* and *Unmasking the Trauma: School Bullying and Children with Special Needs*. Most recently, Dr. Lisbon launched The Burnout Project for special needs moms designed to help moms move from feelings of burnout to feeling refreshed, relaxed, and reenergized. Her vision is to inspire one million families to discover that not only do they have the power to make a difference in their children's lives but also other families raising children with exceptional needs.

## CONNECT WITH THE AUTHOR

Contact: dr.lisbonpeoples@gmail.com

Website: www.advocacycoaching.com
Facebook: www.facebook.com/theadvocacycoach
Twitter: https://twitter.com/raiseurvisions
LinkedIn: www.linkedin.com/in/aprillisbonpeoples

## LEAVE A REVIEW

If you enjoyed this book, please write a review on Amazon and Goodreads! Reviews help authors reach new readers.

Amazon: amazon.com/author/aprillisbon
Goodreads: www.goodreads.com/drapriljlisbon

# REFERENCES

[1] Juvonen, J., & Graham, S. (2014). Bullying in Schools: The Power of Bullies and the Plight of Victims. *Annual Review of Psychology, 65*, 159–185.

[2] Ibid.

[3] Dupper, D. R. (2013). *School Bullying: New Perspectives on a Growing Problem*. Oxford University Press, 8.

[4] Zablotsky, B., Bradshaw, C. P., Anderson, C. M., & Law, P. (2014). Risk Factors for Bullying Among Children with Autism Spectrum Disorders. *Autism, 18*(4), 419–427.

[5] Ibid, 5.

[6] Hall, K., Goldstein, D. M., & Ingram, M. B. (2016). The Hands of Donald Trump: Entertainment, Gesture, Spectacle. *HAU: Journal of Ethnographic Theory, 6*(2), 71–100.

[7] Skiba, R. J., Horner, R. H., Chung, C, Rausch, M. K., May, S. L., & Tobin, T. (2011). Race Is Not Neutral: A National Investigation of African American and Latino Disproportionality in School Discipline. *School Psychology Review, 40*(1), 85–107.

[8] Wright, B. L. (2018). *The Brilliance of Black Boys: Cultivating School Success in the Early Grades.* Teachers College Press.

[9] Blanchett, W. J., Mumford, V., & Beachum, F. (2005). Urban School Failure and Disproportionality in a Post-Brown Era: Benign Neglect of the Constitutional Rights of Students of Color. *Remedial and Special Education, 26*(2), 70–81.

[10] Connor, D. J & Ferri, B. A. (2005). Integration and Inclusion: A troubling Nexus: Race, Disability and Special Education. *The Journal of African American History, 90*(1/2), 107–127.

[11] Skiba, R. J., Michael, R. S., Nardo, A. C., & Peterson, R. (2002). The Color of Discipline: Sources of Racial and Gender Disproportionality in School Punishment. Urban Review, 34, 317–342.

[12] Cramer, E. D., & Bennett, K. D. (2015). Implementing

Culturally Responsive Positive Behavior in Interventions and Supports in Middle School Classrooms. *Middle School Journal.*

[13] Owens, C. M., Ford, D. Y., Lisbon, A. J., & Owens, M. T. (2016). Shifting paradigms to better service twice-exceptional African American Learners. *Behavioral Disorders, 41*(4), 196-208.

[14] Gibson, P.A., Wilson, R., Haight, W., Kayama, M., & Marshall, J. (2014). The Role of Race in the Out-of-School Suspensions of Black Students: The Perspectives of Students with Suspensions, Their Parents and Educators. *Children and Youth Service Review, (47),* 274–282.

[15] Balfanz, R., Byrnes, V., & Fox, J. (2014). Sent Home and Put Off-Track: Antecedents, Disproportionalities, and Consequences of Being Suspended in the Ninth Grade. *Journal of Applied Research on Children: Informing Policy for Children at Risk, 5*(2), 1–21.

[16] Black, A., Giuliano, L., & Narayan, A., (2016). Civil Rights Data Show More Work is Needed to Reduce Inequities in K-12 Schools. Retrieved from: https://obamawhitehouse.archives.gov/blog/2016/12/08/civil-rights-data-show-more-work-needed-reduce-inequities-k-12-schools.

[17] U. S. Department of Education, Office for Civil Rights (2016). Civil Rights Data Collection: A First Look (Data from 2013–2014). Retrieved from

https://www2.ed.gov/about/offices/list/ocr/docs/2013-14-first-look.pdf.

[18] Goff, P. A., Jackson, M. C., Di Leone, B. A. L., Culotta, C. M., & DiTomasso, N. A. (2014). The Essence of Innocence: Consequences of Dehumanizing Black Children. Journal of Personality and Social Psychology, 106(4), 526–545.

[19] Blanchett, W. J. (2006). Disproportionate Representation of African American Students in Special Education: Acknowledging the Role of White Privilege and Racism. *American Educational Research Association, 35*(6), 24–28.

[20] Trenton, L., Marsh, S., & Noguera, P. A. (2017). Beyond Stigma and Stereotypes: An Ethnographic Study on the Effects of School-Imposed Labeling on Black Males in an Urban Charter School. *Urban Review*.

[21] McCray, E. D., & McHatton, P. A. (2011). Less Afraid to Have Them in My Class: Understanding Pre-Service General Educators' Perception about Inclusion. *Teacher Education Quarterly, 38*(4), 135–155.

[22] Lipman, P. (2008). Education Policy, Race, and Neoliberal Urbanism. In S. Greene (Ed.), Literacy as a Civil Right: Reclaiming Social Justice in Literacy Teaching and Learning. New York, NY: Peter Lang, 125–147.

[23] Wright, B. L. (2018). *The Brilliance of Black Boys: Cultivating School Success in the Early Grades.* Teachers College Press.

[24] Skiba, R. J., Simmons, A. B., Ritter, S., Gibb, A. C, Rausch, M. K., Cuadrado, J., Chung, C. (2008). Achieving Equity in Special Education: History, Status, and Current Challenges. *Council for Exceptional Children, 74*(3), 264–288.

[25] McCray, E. D., & McHatton, P. A. (2011). Less Afraid to Have Them in My Class: Understanding Pre-Service General Educators' Perception about Inclusion. *Teacher Education Quarterly, 38*(4), 135–155.

[26] Statts, C. (2014). Implicit Racial Bias and School Discipline Disparities: Exploring the Connection. Kirwan Institute Special Report. Retrieved from: http://kirwaninstitute.osu.edu/wp-content/uploads/2014/05/ki-ib-argument-piece03.pdf.

[27] Wright, B. L. (2018). *The Brilliance of Black Boys: Cultivating School Success in the Early Grades.* Teachers College Press.

[28] Owens, C. M., Ford, D. Y., Lisbon, A. J., & Owens, M. T. (2016). Shifting Paradigms to Better Service Twice-Exceptional African American Learners. *Behavioral Disorders, 41*(4), 196–208.

[29] Skiba, R. J., Michael, R. S., Nardo, A. C., & Peterson, R. (2002). The Color of Discipline: Sources of Racial and

Gender Disproportionality in School Punishment. Urban Review, 34, 317–342.

[30] Skiba, R. J., Horner, R. H., Chung, C, Rausch, M. K., May, S. L., & Tobin, T. (2011). Race Is Not Neutral: A National Investigation of African American and Latino Disproportionality in School Discipline. *School Psychology Review, 40*(1), 85–107.

[31] Goff, P. A., Jackson, M. C., Di Leone, B. A. L., Culotta, C. M., & DiTomasso, N. A. (2014). The Essence of Innocence: Consequences of Dehumanizing Black Children. Journal of Personality and Social Psychology, 106(4), 526–545.

[32] Trenton, L., Marsh, S., & Noguera, P. A. (2017). Beyond Stigma and Stereotypes: An
Ethnographic Study on the Effects of School-Imposed Labeling on Black Males in an Urban Charter School. *Urban Review.*

[33] Welch, K., & Payne, A. A. (2010). Racial Threat and Punitive School Discipline. Social Problems, 57(1), 25–48.

[34] Walker, Kenya (2011). Deficit Thinking and the Effective Teacher. *Education and Urban Society, 43*(5), 576-597.

[35] Ibid, 576–597.

[36] Owens, C. M., Ford, D. Y., Lisbon, A. J., & Owens, M. T.

(2016). Shifting Paradigms to Better Service Twice-Exceptional African American Learners. *Behavioral Disorders, 41*(4), 196-208.

[37] Gibson, P.A., Wilson, R., Haight, W., Kayama, M., & Marshall, J. (2014). The Role of Race in the Out-of-School Suspensions of Black Students: The Perspectives of Students with Suspensions, Their Parents and Educators. *Children and Youth Service Review, (47),* 274–282.

[38] Walker, Kenya (2011). Deficit Thinking and the Effective Teacher. *Education and Urban Society, 43*(5).

[39] Ibid.

[40] Annamma, S. A., Connor, D., Ferri, B. (2013). Dis/Ability Critical Race Studies (Discrit): Theorizing at the Intersections of Race and Dis/Ability. *Race Ethnicity and Education, 16*, 1–31.

[41] Blanchett, W. J., Mumford, V., & Beachum, F. (2005). Urban School Failure and Disproportionality in a Post-Brown Era: Benign Neglect of the Constitutional Rights of Students of Color. *Remedial and Special Education, 26*(2), 70–81.

[42] Ford, D. Y. & Russo, C. J. (2016). Historical and Legal Overview of Special Education Overrepresentation: Access and Equity Denied. *Multiple Voices for Ethnically Diverse Exceptional Learners, 16(1),* 50–57.

[43] Black, A., Giuliano, L., & Narayan, A., (2016). Civil Rights Data Show More Work is Needed to Reduce Inequities in K-12 Schools. Retrieved from: https://obamawhitehouse.archives.gov/blog/2016/12/08/civil-rights-data-show-more-work-needed-reduce-inequities-k-12-schools.

[44] Ford, D. Y. & Russo, C. J. (2016). Historical and Legal Overview of Special Education Overrepresentation: Access and Equity Denied. *Multiple Voices for Ethnically Diverse Exceptional Learners, 16(1)*, 50-57.

[45] Cuevas, R., Ntoumanis, N., Fernandez-Bustos, J. G., & Bartholomew, K. (2018). Does Teacher Evaluation Based on Student Performance Predict Motivation, Well-Being, and Ill-Being? Journal of School Psychology, 68, 154–162.

[46] Katz, J., & Sokal, L. (2016). Universal Design for Learning as a Bridge to Inclusion: A Qualitative Report of Student Voices. *International Journal of Whole Schooling, 12*(2), 36–63.

[47] Wright, B. L. (2018). *The Brilliance of Black Boys: Cultivating School Success in the Early Grades.* Teachers College Press.

[48] Statts, C. (2014). Implicit Racial Bias and School Discipline Disparities: Exploring the Connection. Kirwan Institute Special Report. Retrieved from: http://kirwaninstitute.osu.edu/wp-content/uploads/2014/05/ki-ib-argument-piece03.pdf.

⁴⁹ Ibid.

⁵⁰ Black, A., Giuliano, L., & Narayan, A., (2016). Civil Rights Data Show More Work is Needed to Reduce Inequities in K-12 Schools. Retrieved from: https://obamawhitehouse.archives.gov/blog/2016/12/08/civil-rights-data-show-more-work-needed-reduce-inequities-k-12-schools.

⁵¹ Skiba, R. J., Simmons, A. B., Ritter, S., Gibb, A. C, Rausch, M. K., Cuadrado, J., Chung, C. (2008). Achieving Equity in Special Education: History, Status, and Current Challenges. *Council for Exceptional Children, 74*(3), 264–288.

⁵² Wright, R. A. (2016). Race Matters… And So Does Gender: An Intersectional Examination of Implicit Bias in Ohio School Discipline Disparities. Kirwan Institute. Retrieved from: http://kirwaninstitute.osu.edu/wp-content/uploads/2016/07/Race-matters-and-so-does-Gender.pdf.

⁵³ Welch, K., & Payne, A. A. (2010). Racial Threat and Punitive School Discipline. Social Problems, 57(1), 25–48.

⁵⁴ Blanchett, W. J. (2006). Disproportionate Representation of African American Students in Special Education: Acknowledging the Role of White Privilege and Racism. *American Educational Research Association, 35*(6), 24–28.

[55] Welch, K., & Payne, A. A. (2010). Racial Threat and Punitive School Discipline. Social Problems, 57(1), 25–48.

[56] Skiba, R. J., Simmons, A. B., Ritter, S., Gibb, A. C, Rausch, M. K., Cuadrado, J., Chung, C. (2008). Achieving Equity in Special Education: History, Status, and Current Challenges. *Council for Exceptional Children, 74*(3), 264–288.

[57] Skiba, R. J., Horner, R. H., Chung, C, Rausch, M. K., May, S. L., & Tobin, T. (2011). Race Is Not Neutral: A National Investigation of African American and Latino Disproportionality in School Discipline. *School Psychology Review, 40*(1), 85–107.

[58] Skiba, R. J., Michael, R. S., Nardo, A. C., & Peterson, R. (2002). The Color of Discipline: Sources of Racial and Gender Disproportionality in School Punishment. Urban Review, 34, 317–342.

[59] Ware, F. (2006). Warm Demander Pedagogy: Culturally Responsive Teaching That Supports a Culture of Achievement for African American Students. *Urban Education, 4*(4), 427–456.

www.ingramcontent.com/pod-product-compliance
Lightning Source LLC
Chambersburg PA
CBHW030451010526
44118CB00011B/879